ideals®
THANKSGIVING

Thanksgiving is loved ones
Who come miles and miles
To be greeted with kisses
And welcoming smiles.

Thanksgiving is turkey
And all of the rest
Of the fruits of the harvest
With which we've been blessed.

Thanksgiving is praise
For our Father above,
For His bountiful goodness,
And the gift of His love.

Virginia Blanck Moore

ISBN 0-8249-1030-3 350

Publisher, Patricia A. Pingry
Editor/Ideals, Kathleen S. Pohl
Managing Editor, Marybeth Owens
Art Director, William Scholz
Production Manager, Mark Brunner
Photographic Editor, Gerald Koser
Manuscript Editor, Naomi Galbreath
Research Editor, Linda Robinson

IDEALS—Vol. 41, No. 7 September MCMLXXXIV IDEALS (ISSN 0019-137X) is published eight times a year,
February, March, April, June, August, September, November, December
by IDEALS PUBLISHING CORPORATION, 11315 Watertown Plank Road, Milwaukee, Wis. 53226
Second class postage paid at Milwaukee, Wisconsin and additional mailing offices.
Copyright © MCMLXXXIV by IDEALS PUBLISHING CORPORATION.
POSTMASTER: Send address changes to Ideals, Post Office Box 2100, Milwaukee, Wis. 53201
All rights reserved. Title IDEALS registered U.S. Patent Office.
Published simultaneously in Canada.

ONE YEAR SUBSCRIPTION—eight consecutive issues as published—$15.95
TWO YEAR SUBSCRIPTION—sixteen consecutive issues as published—$27.95
SINGLE ISSUE—$3.50
Outside U.S.A., add $4.00 per subscription year for postage and handling

*Front and
back covers
Fred Dole*

Thanksgiving

The season pours its gifts in lavish measure:
Soil, seed and rain, sunshine through summer days,
Autumn leaves, windsong, the harvest treasure —
So we pour out our muted songs of praise.
Gourds, nuts and fruits are stored in abundance
On cellar shelves where mingled odors cloy;
The autumn wind wafts the subtle fragrance
Of wide-flung harvest fields which we enjoy.
Now garnered in from rows of shining sheaves,
Corn is heaped high as fretted bins will hold;
Just so, little gracious thoughts that leave
Hearts worshipful swell a gratitude untold.
From the bounty of goodness our needs are filled;
And from hearts overflowing is gratitude spilled.

Gloria Ingram Roberts

Photo opposite
HORN OF PLENTY
Fred Sieb

An Autumnal Tonic

What mystery is it? The morning as rare
　　As the Indian Summer may bring!
A tang in the frost and a spice in the air
　　That no city poet can sing!
The crimson and amber and gold of the leaves,
　　As they loosen and flutter and fall
In the path of the park, as it rustlingly weaves
Its way through the maples and under the eaves
　　Of the sparrows that chatter and call.

What hint of delight is it tingles me through? —
　　What vague, indefinable joy?
What yearning for something divine that I knew
　　When a wayward and wood-roving boy?
Aha! and Oho! but I have it, I say —
　　Oh, the mystery brightens at last, —
'Tis the longing and zest of the far, far away,
For a bountiful, old-fashioned dinner today,
　　With the hale harvest-hands of the past.

James Whitcomb Riley

The Reapers Come

Singing, the reapers homeward come, Io! Io!
Merrily singing the harvest home, Io! Io!
Along the field, along the road,
Where autumn is scattering leaves abroad,
Homeward cometh the ripe last load, Io! Io!

Singers are filling the twilight dim
With the cheerful song, Io! Io!
The spirit of song ascends to Him
Who causeth the corn to grow.
He freely sent the gentle rain,
The summer sun glorified hill and plain,
To golden perfection brought the grain, Io! Io!

Silently, nightly, fell the dew,
Gently the rain, Io! Io!
But who can tell how the green corn grew,
Or who beheld it grow?
Oh! God the good, in sun and rain,
He look'd on the flourishing fields and grain,
Till they all appear'd on hill and plain
Like living gold, Io! Io!

Author Unknown

Overleaf
WAGON WHEEL HARVEST
H. Armstrong Roberts

Autumn

Heap high the farmer's wintry hoard!
   Heap high the golden corn!
No richer gift has Autumn poured
   From out her lavish horn.

Let other lands exulting glean
   The apple from the pine,
The orange from its glossy green,
   The cluster from the vine.

But let the good old corn adorn
   The hills our fathers trod;
Still let us, for His golden corn,
   Send up our thanks to God.

John Greenleaf Whittier

Autumnal

When dawn arrives to herald break-of-day,
And tinted glow of morning greets the eyes,
The quiet hush — with never long to stay —
Is broken by wind brooms that sweep the skies.
And seasons then enforce their agelong hold
And grant the deed to which they each give birth,
As in the summer change to autumn gold
I see the tasseled harvest gift of earth.

May God forbid! that all this beauty lie
Nor fan emotions' flame at early dawn —
While words that former years allowed to die
Remain still dormant, with no chance to spawn.

For there can be no joy without this hour
When all the verdant earth begins to flower.

Howard A. Dettmers

Thanks

Thank you very much indeed,
River, for your waving reed;
Hollyhocks, for budding knobs;
Foxgloves, for your velvet fobs;
Pansies, for your silky cheeks;
Chaffinches, for singing beaks;
Spring, for wood anemones
Near the mossy toes of trees;
Summer, for the fruited pear,
Yellowing crab, and cherry fare;
Autumn, for the bearded load,
Hazelnuts along the road;
Winter, for the fairy tale,
Spitting log and bouncing hail.

But, blest Father, high above,
All these joys are from Thy love;
And Your children, everywhere,
Born in palace, lane, or square,
Cry with voices all agreed,
"Thank You very much indeed."

Norman Gale

November

When thistle-blows do lightly float
About the pasture height,
And shrills the hawk a parting note,
And creeps the frost at night,
Then hilly ho! though singing so,
And whistle as I may,
There comes again the old heart pain
Through all the livelong day.

In high wind creaks the leafless tree
And nods the fading fern;
The knolls are dun as snow-clouds be,
And cold the sun does burn.
Then ho, hollo! though calling so,
I cannot keep it down;
The tears arise unto my eyes,
And thoughts are chill and brown.

Far in the cedars' dusky stoles,
Where the sere ground-vine weaves,
The partridge drums funereal rolls
Above the fallen leaves.
And hip, hip, ho! though cheering so,
It stills no whit the pain;
For drip, drip, drip, from bare branch tip,
I hear the year's last rain.

So drive the cold cows from the hill,
And call the wet sheep in;
And let their stamping clatter fill
The barn with warming din.
And ho, folk, ho! though it be so
That we no more may roam,
We still will find a cheerful mind
Around the fire at home!

C. L. Cleaveland

Father,
We Thank Thee

For flowers that bloom about our feet,
   Father, we thank Thee,
For tender grass so fresh and sweet,
   Father, we thank Thee,
For the song of bird and hum of bee,
For all things fair we hear or see,
Father in heaven, we thank Thee.

For blue of stream and blue of sky,
   Father, we thank Thee.
For pleasant shade of branches high,
   Father, we thank Thee.
For fragrant air and cooling breeze,
For beauty of the blooming trees,
Father in heaven, we thank Thee.

For this new morning with its light,
   Father, we thank Thee,
For rest and shelter of the night,
   Father, we thank Thee,
For health and food, for love and friends,
For everything Thy goodness sends,
Father in heaven, we thank Thee.

Ralph Waldo Emerson

Photo opposite
MUMS AND ORNAMENTAL CABBAGE
H. Armstrong Roberts

New England November

In that New Haven house
Where laughing relatives
Perform the family jokes
And all the family lives,

Where turkey roasted whole,
Potatoes, turnips, peas,
Onions and Brussels sprouts,
And globes of Holland cheese,

Where pumpkin, apples, mince
And seven kinds of pie,
Plum pudding, cake and nuts,
Fill up the family eye;

Or in that northern house
Where two old people stay,
Valley'd between red hills
That burn the sky away,

And stuff their cellar full
Of food won by the hand
In years of labouring
On the New Hampshire land;

That country now is full
Of fire and plenteousness,
And pride blesses the land;
The land that comes back to bless.

Donald Hall

November

November marks the falling leaves,
The fodder cut and bound in sheaves,
The acorns falling to the ground,
Pheasants making a cautious sound,

A hunter's moon across the sky,
Flocks of wild geese flying high,
And squirrels in their leafy towers
All snug against November showers

When rain turns sleet and sleet turns snow —
That is the way the seasons go.
With winter weather on the way
There still remains Thanksgiving Day.

It is our nation's famed repast —
November saves the best till last —
And fields and woods and leaf and tree
All join in the festivity.

Minnie Klemme

Thanksgiving Time

The autumn season finishes the year,
Hangs harvest moon in a cooler atmosphere.
Grain ripens: wheat and oats leap into shocks,
We hasten toward the year's last equinox!
Now winter hides behind a northern sky,
Floats in each wavering wind that flurries by.
Thanksgiving time, corn hurries toward the barn,
As ice forms isles on meadow brook and tarn.
At borderland of every fertile field,
Marauding crows peck at remaining yield
Of grain, dropped by machine or man, unseen...
They chatter as they sweep the furrows clean.
Apples, like small red worlds, plunge down
   the night
On orchards, in mounds beautiful and bright.
Fall changes little as the years swing by —
The prairie folk are glad...and so am I!
For every single blessing gives a reason
That we rejoice at this Thanksgiving season!

Stella Craft Tremble

Autumn Pastries

Cranberry-Pineapple Pie

1 pound fresh cranberries
1 can (6½ ounces) pineapple chunks, drained
1 cup pineapple juice
2 cups sugar
    Juice of 1 lemon
2 tablespoons unflavored gelatin
1 9-inch pie shell, baked
    Whipped cream

Bring cranberries, pineapple, pineapple juice, sugar, lemon juice, and gelatin to a boil. Boil 10 minutes. Cool. Pour into pie shell and chill. Garnish with whipped cream.

Plantation Pecan Pie

3 eggs
1 cup light corn syrup
½ cup sugar
¼ cup butter *or* margarine, melted
1 teaspoon vanilla
1 cup pecan halves
1 9-inch pieshell, unbaked

Preheat oven to 350° F. In a medium bowl, beat eggs thoroughly with a wire whisk or hand beater. Beat in corn syrup, sugar, butter, and vanilla until well blended. Arrange pecan halves in a single layer in bottom of piecrust. Pour egg mixture carefully over the pecans. Bake 1 hour or until knife inserted about 1 inch from the edge comes out clean. Cool.

Coconut-Pumpkin Pie

1 can (3½ ounces) flaked coconut, divided
¼ cup crushed graham cracker crumbs
⅓ cup butter *or* margarine, melted
2 tablespoons sugar
1 envelope unflavored gelatin
¾ teaspoon cinnamon
½ teaspoon ground ginger
½ teaspoon nutmeg
½ teaspoon salt
¾ cup sugar, divided
3 eggs, separated
½ cup milk
1¼ cups canned pumpkin
    Whipped cream

Preheat oven to 375° F. Spread coconut on a cookie sheet; bake 8 to 10 minutes or until lightly browned. Reserve two tablespoons for garnish. In a 9-inch pie plate, mix remaining coconut, crumbs, butter, and 2 tablespoons sugar. Press firmly to bottom and side of pie plate. Bake for 7 minutes or until golden. Set aside to cool. In the top of a double boiler, blend gelatin, cinnamon, ginger, nutmeg, salt, and ½ cup sugar. In a small bowl, beat egg yolks with milk until blended. Stir into gelatin mixture. Blend in pumpkin. Cook over boiling water, stirring often, for 20 minutes or until thickened. Refrigerate until cool but not set. In a large bowl, beat egg whites until soft peaks form. Continue to beat at high speed while sprinkling in remaining ¼ cup sugar. Gently fold pumpkin mixture into beaten egg whites. Pour into crust; refrigerate until set. Serve topped with whipped cream and a sprinkling of toasted coconut.

Photo opposite
AUTUMN PASTRIES
Gerald Koser

Thanksgiving Memories

How dearly I remember
Those long vanished frosty morns
When the smells from Grandma's kitchen
Told Thanksgiving Day was born;
When children gazed with wonder
That they scarcely could disguise
At a plump and fragrant turkey
And a wealth of pumpkin pies.

Brian F. King

JOHN SLOBODNIK

Children's Hour

Clasp the hands,
Bow the head,
Ask the Lord
To bless the bread.
Pull the chair
Up to the table;
Eat as much
As you are able.
Lend a kindly
Ear to Papa;
Save the scraps
For kitty's supper.
Clear the dishes,
Help your mother;
Be sweet and good
To one another.
Then for this day,
Serene, unprankful,
All parents will be
Truly thankful.

Grace Tall

Thanksgiving

The turkey is roasted;
The cranberry's sweet;
The table is laden
With good things to eat.

The family is seated,
Each one in his place;
Heads bow for the blessing,
For silence and grace.

There's fellowship, laughter,
And hearts are so gay;
There's gratitude, gladness,
On Thanksgiving Day.

Esther F. Thom

Thanksgiving Wishes

Like the harvest horn of plenty
Spilling out its fruit and grain,
May Thanksgiving tumble blessings
On your household once again.

May your turkey be the plumpest,
Roasted to a golden brown,
And your pies of mince and pumpkin
Waft their spices through the town.

May your guests be laughter-loving,
With contentment in their eyes,
And the youngsters filled with wonder
At each gourmet surprise.

Then when the day is over
And it's time for guests to part,
May the spirit of Thanksgiving
Linger still within your heart.

Kay Grayman Parker

For Small Blessings

Today I offer thanks — not for great things
So graciously bestowed, but for such small
Shy things as violets by an old stone wall,
Pink peach bloom, and the whir of bright-hued wings;
For balm of tender green that heals the scars
Of winter, crimson buds of maple trees;
The first arbutus and anemones
Sprinkling the woods with delicate, fragrant stars.

For furry kittens, downy soft and white,
Snuggling close by in trusting, warm content;
Purring their thanks for tiny blessings sent
Of bread and milk, with golden eyes alight;
Days that go smoothly without fear or fret,
Anxiety or grief, to mar their calm;
And nights of peaceful rest, that like a psalm,
Courage and strength for the new day beget.

Majestic mountain height and billowing sea,
Wide prairies that outreach the sight of man,
Stark, frigid wastes defying human span,
Afford us moments of rare ecstasy;
And for them it is meet we bring our praise.
But just today I offered thanks for small
And simple things, familiar to us all —
The take-for-granted things of common days.

Jessie Wilmore Murton

Photo opposite
FALL BOUNTY
Gerald Koser

Thanksgiving Day

Golden pumpkins on the vine,
Corn stalks tall and brown,
Jack Frost's icy footprints
Scattered on the ground;

Apples polished red and shiny,
'Taters in the bin,
Now's the time to thank our Lord
For the harvest gathered in.

The table's full of goodies;
Our hearts are full of love;
We give our thanks to you, Lord,
For blessings from above.

Thanksgiving Day is here again
And let us be aware
That with its fun and gaiety
It's first a day of prayer.

Lois Groover

Thanksgiving

'Twas this the mother always said:
"Be thankful for your daily bread
And thankful for your strength to bear
Whatever comes of hurt and care.

"Make every day Thanksgiving Day!
At table bow your heads and pray
And give your hearts to God above
In gratitude for all His love.

"Be thankful for the loveliness
Of earth in every season's dress;
The springtime green, the summer rose,
And autumn's glorious, golden close.

"Be thankful for your blessings all:
The happy memories you recall:
For Time, which every heartache mends
And, oh, be thankful for your friends!"

Edgar A. Guest

A Psalm of Thanks

O give thanks unto the Lord; for he is good:
For his mercy endureth forever.
O give thanks unto the God of gods:
For his mercy endureth forever.
O give thanks to the Lord of lords:
For his mercy endureth forever.

To him who alone doeth great wonders:
For his mercy endureth forever.
To him that by wisdom made the heavens:
For his mercy endureth forever.
To him that stretched out the earth above the waters:
For his mercy endureth forever.
To him that made great lights:
For his mercy endureth forever.
The sun to rule by day:
For his mercy endureth forever.
The moon and stars to rule by night:
For his mercy endureth forever.

O give thanks unto the God of heaven:
For his mercy endureth forever.

Psalm 136

Come, Ye Thankful People

HENRY ALFORD   GEORGE ELVEY

1. Come, ye thank-ful peo-ple, come,   Raise the song of har-vest home:
2. All the world is God's own field,   Fruit un-to His praise to yield;
3. For the Lord our God shall come,   And shall take His har-vest home;
4. E-ven so, Lord, quick-ly come   To Thy fi-nal har-vest home;

All is safe-ly gath-ered in,   Ere the win-ter storms be-gin;
Wheat and tares to-geth-er sown,   Un-to joy or sor-row grown;
From His field shall in that day   All of-fens-es purge a-way;
Gath-er Thou Thy peo-ple in,   Free from sor-row, free from sin;

God, our Ma-ker, doth pro-vide For our wants to be sup-plied:
First the blade, and then the ear, Then the full corn shall ap-pear:
Give His an-gels charge at last In the fire the tares to cast;
There, for-ev-er pu-ri-fied, In Thy pres-ence to a-bide:

Come to God's own tem-ple, come, Raise the song of har-vest home.
Lord of har-vest, grant that we Whole-some grain and pure may be.
But the fruit-ful ears to store In His gar-ner ev-er-more.
Come, with all Thine an-gels, come, Raise the glo-rious har-vest home.

We Gather Together

Translated from the Dutch by THEODORE BAKER   Traditional tune arranged by EDWARD KREMSER

1. We gath-er to - geth-er to ask the Lord's bless-ing;
2. Be - side us to guide us, our God with us join-ing,
3. We all do ex - tol Thee, Thou Lead - er tri - um-phant,

He chas-tens and has-tens His will to make known;
Or - dain - ing, main-tain-ing His king-dom di - vine;
And pray that Thou still our De - fend - er wilt be.

The wick - ed op - press-ing now cease from dis - tress-ing;
So from the be - gin-ning the fight we were win-ning;
Let Thy con-gre - ga - tion es - cape trib - u - la-tion;

Sing prais - es to His Name, He for-gets not His own.
Thou, Lord, wast at our side, all glo - ry be Thine.
Thy Name be ev - er praised! O Lord, Make us free! A - men.

New England Thanksgiving

The king and high priest of all festivals was the autumn Thanksgiving. When the apples were all gathered and the cider was all made, and the yellow pumpkins were rolled in from many a hill in billows of gold, and the corn was husked, and the labors of the season were done, and the warm, late days of Indian Summer came in, dreamy, and calm, and still, with just enough frost to crisp the ground of a morning, but with warm traces of benignant, sunny hours at noon, there came over the community a sort of genial repose of spirit, — a sense of something accomplished, and of a new golden mark made in advance, — and the deacon began to say to the minister, of a Sunday, "I suppose it's about time for the Thanksgiving proclamation."

Harriet Beecher Stowe

Photo opposite
COUNTRY CHURCH
Chelsea, Vermont
Bob Clemenz

Thanksgiving Memories

by Gladys Taber

After Thanksgiving dinner, the house simmers down to quiet. It seems cosy and natural to hear muted voices from all over, the baby upstairs waking up, Connie and Don talking, Don's wife tuning the guitar and humming. With all the food around, I reflect comfortably, we won't need to get another sit-down meal, they can raid.

Naturally in a very few hours, there is a kind of stir.

"When are we going to eat?"

"Is it almost supper time?"

"Mind if I eat a little more chestnut stuffing?"

It is very much as it was on Christmas when I said to Jill, "We can have the leftover turkey tomorrow," and she said, "What turkey?"

It turns out there is just enough to slice thin and have cold, plus extra dressing, and reinforced with a casserole of home-baked beans nobody perishes of starvation.

"And all of them as thin as pencils," I mourn afterward, "it just isn't fair! They can just eat alarmingly and never gain an ounce. Whereas I — no, no justice at all."

Thanksgiving is far more than the family dinner and national festival. I know all people have always had harvest celebrations of one kind or another, so there is nothing distinctive about a feast time after the crops are in. But our Thanksgiving seems very close to our relation with God. It has a deep religious significance not always spoken of, but, I think, felt.

I like to slip away for a brief time and sit by the pond on the one bench left out all winter. If it is a warm hazy day, the sun is slanting over the hill with a gentle glow. If it is cold, the wind walks in the woods. I think of everything I have to be thankful for, and it is a long list by the time it is added up. I am thankful for love, and friends, and the family gathering together. For starlight over the old apple orchard. For the chilly sweetness of peepers in April. For my winter birds, so brave, so hungry, particularly for my little chickadee with the bent wing that bangs away at the suet cake right while I type. He cocks a shining eye at me and seems to say, "Life is really what you make of it, eh?"

I am thankful for music and books. And for the dogs barking at the gate. Well, there are so many things to be thankful for that the list is infinitely long.

And it is good to take time to be thankful, for it is all too easy to let the world's trouble sweep over one in a dark flood and to fall into despair.

Overleaf
FALL FARMLANDS
Peacham, Vermont
Bob Clemenz

Indian Summer

These are the days when birds come back,
A very few, a bird or two,
To take a backward look.

These are the days when skies put on
The old, old sophistries of June —
A blue and gold mistake.

Ah, fraud that cannot cheat the bee,
Almost thy plausibility
Induces my belief,

Till ranks of seeds their witness bear,
And softly through the altered air
Hurries a timid leaf!

Oh, sacrament of summer days,
Oh, last communion in the haze,
Permit a child to join,

Thy sacred emblems to partake,
Thy consecrated bread to break,
Taste thine immortal wine!

Emily Dickinson

Indian Summer

The leaves borne high upon the breeze
Are lifeless tans and browns
That only lately clothed the trees
In red and orange gowns.
And on the hills the cattle graze
Content in Indian summer haze.

No birdsong now at eventide
Pervades the twilight calm;
A peace rests on the countryside —
A soft unspoken psalm.
A lilac haze enwraps the hills
And hovers over wayward rills.

The sun looks ghostly through a veil
Of Indian summer weather,
Its glowing face, an eerie pale,
Fires neither hedge nor heather.
O lovely season, witching, wan,
I would that it might linger on!

Maude Woods Plessinger

Chrysanthemums

With summer and sun behind you,
 With winter and shade before,
You crowd in your regal splendor
 Through the autumn's closing door.
White as the snow that is coming,
 Red as the rose that is gone,
Gold as the heart of the lilies,
 Pink as the flush of the dawn.
Confident, winsome, stately,
 You throng in the wane of the year,
Trooping an army with banners
 When the leafless woods are sere.

Sweet is your breath as of spices
 From a far sea island blown;
Chaste your robes as of vestals
 Trimming their lamps alone.
Strong are your hearts, and sturdy
 The life that in root and stem
Smoulders and glows till it sparkles
 In each flowery diadem.
Nothing of bloom and odor
 Have your peerless legions lost,
Marching in fervid beauty
 To challenge the death-white frost.

So to the eye of sorrow
 Ye bring a flicker of light;
The cheek that was wan with illness
 Smiles at your faces bright.
The children laugh in greeting,
 And the dear old people say,
"Here are the selfsame darlings
 We loved in our own young day,"
As, summer and sun behind you,
 Winter and shade before,
You crowd in your regal splendor
 Through the autumn's closing door.

Margaret Elizabeth Sangster

Readers' Reflections

The Harvest

The harvest has been gathered in,
A great round moon rides high,
The night winds tell old Mother Earth
The time to rest is nigh.

A cloak of gold and scarlet
Is draped across the hills;
Soon trees will scatter leaves about
As autumn nights grow chill.

The wildlings have a secret place
For storing food they've found;
Each tree house will be snug and warm
When winter comes around.

The bounty of the rich dark earth
Has proved a mighty yield:
A lavish cornucopia
From orchard, vine, and field.

Mildred L. Jarrell

It's Thanksgiving Time

At Thanksgiving time
We're ready to go
To grandfather's house.
How we hope it will snow!

Our cousins and uncles
And aunts all come, too;
And everyone helps,
For there's so much to do.

We set the long table
With cloth snowy white,
And an autumn bouquet
That is cheery and bright.

If there's snow, we all pile
In the big two-horse sleigh
For a ride, with bells jingling,
On Thanksgiving Day!

Jessie Wilmore Murton

Thanksgiving

Faith made visible
In daily living:
The perfect gift
Of a grateful heart.

Florine H. Robinson

Editor's Note: Readers are invited to submit poetry, short anecdotes, and humorous reflections on life for possible publication in future *Ideals* issues. Writers will receive $10 for each published submission. Send material to "Readers' Reflections," P.O. Box 1101, Milwaukee, Wisconsin 53201.

Thanksgiving Harvest

Not only am I thankful for
The fields of ripened grain
And cellars that are filled with food
For wintertime again,

But also I am filled with thanks
For friends who've come my way
To add their special touch of peace
And beauty to the day.

The harvest of kind words and deeds,
The strength that comes from friends,
The chance to give and to receive:
All bring joy without end.

Thanksgiving calls me to assess
The value of a smile,
The ripening fellowships I share,
The friends across the miles.

Craig E. Sathoff

Thanksgiving at the Farm

The kitchen stove is throwing out its heat,
And there are smells of such good things to eat:
The roasting turkey, mince and pumpkin pies,
A chocolate cake, and jelly tarts to prize.

Outside, the children run around at play
Filled with excitement of this holiday;
Women are chatting about homely things
While menfolk talk of what each season brings

To fertile acres now all harvested.
The dishes are brought out, the cloth is spread;
And when the family is gathered there,
Each head is gravely bowed in simple prayer

Of thankfulness for all that earth bestows,
Abundant treasure before winter snows.

Louise Darcy

Happy Thanksgiving

I bring Thanksgiving greetings,
The warmest wishes, too,
Because you've made me thankful
To have a friend like you!

Reginald Holmes

Turn Around

The leaves are falling —
Earth leans into winter
Half asleep;
The sun still burns
With a thousand fires,
Reaching the world
Through cloud-corners.
Dry vines rasp
Against barrier glass.
Bees vanish in one day.
Only the dragonfly remains
Darting off the hollow edge
Of final summer.
An owl sits alone,
Inscrutable,
Owning the world.
Stars, winds, and nights are his.

The leaves are falling,
Having lived their measured time.
Wild geese angle the evening sky
Calling age-old verities.

Spellbound by one robin's mirth,
I feel the music of the spinning earth.

Evelyn G. Kozma

Thanksgiving Philosophy

"Hiss! Hiss!" said the Goose, "they've taken us three
To fatten for Christmas — such songsters we!
I'll be tough as a goose! It's a sin and a shame.
Be wise, Mister Turkey, and you'll do the same.
            Hiss!" said the Goose,
            "I call it abuse!"
            "Quack!" said the Duck,
            "I call it good luck!
Just think of the dainties they give us to eat —
Such apple cores, squash seeds, and gristles of meat!
Let's be off for a lunch; see how fast I can hobble."
But the Turkey only answered with a
            "Gobble! gobble! gobble!"

"Hiss! Hiss!" said the Goose, " 'tis a sad want of luck!
You don't know a thing; you're a goose of a duck!
A regular quack, — you haven't any brains;
You don't know enough to go in when it rains."
            "Quack!" said the Duck,
            " 'Tis a world of good luck!"
            "Hiss!" said the Goose,
            " 'Tis a world of abuse!"
"Quack! quack!" said the Duck, "what a great goose you are."
"Hiss!" shrilled the Goose, till you heard her afar,
"Hiss! Mister Turkey, the world is full of trouble."
But the Turkey only answered with a
            "Gobble! gobble! gobble!"

Charlotte W. Thurston

Wheatfield Friend

Scarecrow in the wheatfield,
Making friends of crows —
He's stuffed with straw and buttoned up
Against the coming snows.

He has a pumpkin for a head
With Grandad's hat on top;
His outstretched arms reach out to squirrels
And cottontails that hop.

With friendly smile and wrinkled brow,
And triangle-twinkling eyes,
He watches while the seasons change
Beneath the autumn skies.

Susan Halderson Baker

Photo opposite
WHEATFIELD FRIEND
Bob Taylor

GOODY O'GRUMPITY

When Goody O'Grumpity baked a cake
The tall reeds danced by the mournful lake,
The pigs came nuzzling out of their pens,
The dogs ran sniffing and so did the hens,
And the children flocked by dozens and tens.
They came from the north, the east and the south
With wishful eyes and watering mouth,
And stood in a crowd about Goody's door,
Their muddy feet on her sanded floor.
And what do you s'pose they came to do!
Why, to lick the dish when Goody was through!
And throughout the land went such a smell
Of citron and spice — no words can tell
How cinnamon bark and lemon rind,
And round, brown nutmegs grated fine
A wonderful haunting perfume wove,
Together with allspice, ginger and clove,
When Goody but opened the door of her stove.
The children moved close in a narrowing ring,
They were hungry — as hungry as bears in the spring;
They said not a word, just breathed in the spice,
And at last when the cake was all golden and nice,
Goody took a great knife and cut each a slice.

Carol Ryrie Brink

Originally printed in *Story Parade*. Reprinted with permission of Nora C. Hunter and David R. Brink.

Giving Thanks

For the hay and the corn and wheat that is
   reaped,
For the labor well done, and the barns that are
   heaped,
For the sun and the dew and the sweet
   honeycomb,
For the rose and the song, and the harvest
   brought home —
      Thanksgiving! Thanksgiving!
For the trade and the skill and the wealth in
   our land,
For the cunning and strength of the working-
   man's hand,
For the good that our artists and poets have
   taught,
For the friendship that hope and affection have
   brought —
      Thanksgiving! Thanksgiving!
For the homes that with purest affection are
   blest,
For the season of plenty and well deserved rest,
For our country extending from sea to sea,
The land that is known as the "Land of the
   Free" —
      Thanksgiving! Thanksgiving!

Author Unknown

The First Thanksgiving Day

In Puritan New England a year had passed
   away
Since first beside the Plymouth coast the
   English Mayflower lay,
When Bradford, the good Governor, sent fowlers
   forth to snare
The turkey and the wildfowl, to increase the
   scanty fare:

"Our husbandry hath prospered, there is corn
   enough for food,
Though 'the pease be parched in blossom, and
   the grain indifferent good.'
Who blessed the loaves and fishes for the feast
   miraculous,
And filled with oil the widow's cruse, He hath
   remembered us!

"Give thanks unto the Lord of Hosts, by whom
   we all are fed,
Who granted us our daily prayer, 'Give us our
   daily bread!'
By us and by our children let this day be kept
   for aye,
In memory of His bounty, as the land's
   Thanksgiving Day."

Each brought his share of Indian meal the
   pious feast to make,
With the fat deer from the forest and the
   wildfowl from the brake.
And chanted hymn and prayer were raised —
   though eyes with tears were dim —
"The Lord He hath remembered us, let us
   remember Him!"

Then Bradford stood up at their head and lifted
    up his voice:
"The corn is gathered from the field, I call you
    to rejoice;
Thank God for all His mercies, from the greatest
    to the least,
Together we have fasted, friends, together let
    us feast.

"The Lord who led forth Israel was with us in
    the waste:
Sometime in light, sometime in cloud, before us
    He hath paced;
Now give Him thanks, and pray to Him who
    holds us in His hand
To prosper us and make of this a strong and
    mighty land!"

From Plymouth to the Golden Gate today
    their children tread,
The mercies of that bounteous Hand
    upon the land are shed;
The "flocks are on a thousand hills," the prairies
    wave with grain,
The cities spring like mushrooms now where
    once was desert plain.

Heap high the board with plenteous cheer and
    gather to the feast,
And toast that sturdy Pilgrim band whose
    courage never ceased.
Give praise to that All-Gracious One by whom
    their steps were led,
And thanks unto the harvest's Lord who sends
    our "daily bread."

Alice Williams Brotherton

The First Thanksgiving

Indian summer soon came in a blaze of glory, and it was time to bring in the crops. All in all, their first harvest was a disappointment. Their twenty acres of corn, thanks to Squanto, had done well enough. But the Pilgrims failed miserably with the more familiar crops.... Still, it was possible to make a substantial increase in the individual weekly food ration which for months had consisted merely of a peck of meal from the stores brought on the Mayflower. This was doubled by adding a peck of maize a week, and the company decreed a holiday so that all might, "after a more special manner, rejoyce together."

The Pilgrims had other things to be thankful for. They had made peace with the Indians and walked "as peaceably and safely in the woods as in the highways of England." A start had been made in the beaver trade. There had been no sickness for months. Eleven houses now lined the street — seven private dwellings and four buildings for common use. There had been no recurrence of mutiny and dissension. Faced with common dangers, Saints and Strangers had drawn closer together, sinking doctrinal differences for a time....

As the day of the harvest approached, four men were sent out to shoot waterfowl, returning with enough to supply the company for a week. Massasoit was invited to attend and shortly arrived — with ninety ravenous braves! The strain on the larder was somewhat eased when some of these went out and bagged five deer. Captain Standish staged a military review, there were games of skill and chance, and for three days the Pilgrims and their guests gorged themselves on venison, roast duck, roast goose, clams and other shellfish, succulent eels, white bread, corn bread, leeks and watercress, and other "sallet herbes," with wild plums and dried berries as dessert — all washed down with wine, made of the wild grape both white and red, which the Pilgrims praised as "very sweet and strong." At this first Thanksgiving feast in New England the company may have enjoyed, though there is no mention of it in the record, some of the long-legged "turkies" whose speed of foot in the woods constantly amazed the Pilgrims. And there were cranberries in neighboring bogs....

The celebration was a great success, warmly satisfying to body and soul alike, and the Pilgrims held another the next year, repeating it more or less regularly for generations.

George F. Willison

From SAINTS AND STRANGERS, copyright 1945 by George F. Willison. Reprinted with permission of Florence H. Willison.

Thanksgiving in Boston Harbor

"Praise ye the Lord!" The psalm today
Still rises on our ears,
Borne from the hills of Boston Bay
Through five times fifty years,
When Winthrop's fleet from Yarmouth crept
Out to the open main,
And through the widening waters swept,
In April sun and rain.
   "Pray to the Lord with fervent lips,"
   The leader shouted, "pray";
   And prayer arose from all the ships
   As faded Yarmouth Bay.

They passed the Scilly Isles that day,
And May days came, and June,
And thrice upon the ocean lay
The full orb of the moon.
And as that day, on Yarmouth Bay,
Ere England sunk from view,
While yet the rippling Solent lay
In April skies of blue,
   "Pray to the Lord with fervent lips,"
   Each morn was shouted, "pray";
   And prayer arose from all the ships,
   As first in Yarmouth Bay;

Blew warm the breeze o'er Western seas,
Through Maytime morns, and June,
Till hailed these souls the Isles of Shoals,
Low 'neath the summer moon;
And as Cape Ann arose to view,
And Norman's Woe they passed,
The wood doves came the white mists through,
And circled round each mast.
   "Pray to the Lord with fervent lips,"
   Then called the leader, "pray";
   And prayer arose from all the ships,
   As first in Yarmouth Bay.

Above the sea the hill-tops fair —
God's towers — began to rise,
And odors rare breathe through the air,
Like balms of Paradise.
Through burning skies the ospreys flew,
And near the pine-cooled shores
Danced airy boat and thin canoe,
To flash of sunlit oars.
   "Pray to the Lord with fervent lips,"
   The leader shouted, "pray!"
   Then prayer arose, and all the ships
   Sailed into Boston Bay.

The white wings folded, anchors down,
The sea-worn fleet in line,
Fair rose the hills where Boston town
Should rise from clouds of pine;
Fair was the harbor, summit-walled,
And placid lay the sea.
"Praise ye the Lord," the leader called;
"Praise ye the Lord," spake he.
   "Give thanks to God with fervent lips,
   Give thanks to God today,"
   The anthem rose from all the ships,
   Safe moored in Boston Bay.

Our fathers' prayers have changed to psalms,
As David's treasures old
Turned, on the Temple's giant arms,
To lily-work of gold.
Ho! vanished ships from Yarmouth's tide,
Ho! ships of Boston Bay,
Your prayers have crossed the centuries wide
To this Thanksgiving Day!
   We pray to God with fervent lips,
   We praise the Lord today,
   As prayers arose from Yarmouth ships,
   But psalms from Boston Bay.

Hezekiah Butterworth

Margaret Elizabeth Sangster

Margaret Elizabeth Sangster was a precocious youngster who, by the time she was four, could read "almost any book." She was born in 1838 in New Rochelle, New York, and grew up in New York City and in New Jersey.

Throughout her childhood and school days she filled her notebooks with verses and essays that reflected her practical and religious attitudes toward life. At seventeen her first of many stories was published. But not until she found herself a young widow with a child to support did she turn to writing seriously, hoping to find in it a source of income.

Freelance assignments soon led to editorial positions on prominent children's, Christian, and family magazines. In 1889, Mrs. Sangster was appointed editor of *Harper's Bazaar,* a position she held for ten years, until the magazine's demise. While editor at *Harper's,* she also wrote several novels as well as articles and verse for leading women's magazines.

Her verse reflects the American character, a Christian outlook, and her genuine concern for the welfare of children and young women. Her work has found a wide and admiring audience.

The Child and the Bird

"Oh, where are you going, my dear little bird?
And why do you hurry away?
Not a leaf on the pretty red maple has stirred
In the sweet golden sunshine today."

"I know, little maiden, the sunshine is bright,
And the leaves are asleep on the tree,
But three times the dream of a cold winter's night
Has come to my children and me.

"So, good-bye to you, darling, for off we must go
To the land where the oranges bloom,
For we birdies would freeze in the storms and the snow
And forget how to sing in the gloom."

"Will you ever come back to your own little nest?"
"Ah, yes, when the blossoms are here,
We'll return to the orchard we all love the best,
And then we will sing to you, dear."

Pumpkin Pie

Through sun and shower the pumpkin grew
When the days were long and the skies were blue.

And it felt quite vain when its giant size
Was such that it carried away the prize

At the County Fair, when the people came;
And it wore a ticket and bore a name.

Alas for the pumpkin's pride! One day
A boy and his mother took it away.

It was pared and sliced, and pounded and stewed,
And the way it was treated was harsh and rude.

It was sprinkled with sugar and seasoned with spice;
The boy and his mother pronounced it nice.

It was served in a paste, it was baked and browned,
And at last on a pantry shelf was found.

And on Thursday John and Mary and Mabel
Will see it on aunty's laden table.

For the pumpkin grew 'neath a summer sky
Just to turn at Thanksgiving into pie.

Thanksgiving

What time the latest flower hath bloomed,
   The latest bird hath southward flown;
When silence weaves o'er garnered sheaves
   Sweet idylls in our northern zone;
When scattered children rest beside
   The hearth and hold the mother's hand,
Then rolls Thanksgiving's ample tide
   Of fervent praise across the land.

And though the autumn stillness broods
   Where spring was glad with song and stir,
Though summer's grace leave little trace
   On fields that smiled at sight of her,
Still glows the sunset's altar fire
   With crimson flame and heart of gold,
And faith uplifts, with strong desire
   And deep content, the hymns of old.

We bless our God for wondrous wealth,
   Through all the bright benignant year;
For shower and rain, for ripened grain;
   For gift and guerdon, far and near.
We bless the ceaseless Providence
   That watched us through the peaceful days,
That led us home or brought us thence,
   And kept us in our various ways.

And if the hand so much that gave
   Hath something taken from our store,
If caught from sight to heaven's pure light,
   Some precious ones are here no more,
We still adore the Friend above,
   Who, while earth's road grows steep and dim,
Yet comforts us in tender love,
   And holds our darlings close to Him.

Thanks, then, O God! From sea to sea
   Let every wind the anthem bear!
And hearts be rife through toil and strife,
   With joyful praise and grateful prayer.
Our fathers' God, their children sing
   The grace they sought through storm and sun;
Our harvest tribute here we bring,
   And end it with, "Thy will be done."

Nature's Blessings

Still later in the season Nature's tenderness waxes stronger. It is impossible not to be fond of our mother now; for she is so fond of us! At other periods she does not make this impression on me, or only at rare intervals; but in these genial days of autumn, when she has perfected her harvests and accomplished every needful thing that was given her to do, then she overflows with a blessed superfluity of love. She has leisure to caress her children now. It is good to be alive at such times. Thank Heaven for breath — yes, for mere breath — when it is made up of a heavenly breeze like this! It comes with a real kiss upon our cheeks; it would linger fondly around us if it might; but since it must be gone, it embraces us with its whole kindly heart and passes onward to embrace likewise the next thing that it meets. A blessing is flung abroad and scattered far and wide over the earth, to be gathered up by all who choose. I recline upon the still unwithered grass and whisper to myself, "O perfect day! O beautiful world! O beneficent God!" And it is the promise of a blessed eternity; for our Creator would never have made such lovely days and have given us the deep hearts to enjoy them, above and beyond all thought, unless we were meant to be immortal. This sunshine is the golden pledge thereof. It beams through the gates of paradise and shows us glimpses far inward.

Nathaniel Hawthorne

Photo opposite
WEBBED WONDER
Ina Mackey

An Autumn Garden

My tent stands in a garden
Of aster and goldenrod,
Tilled by the rain and the sunshine,
And sown by the hand of God, —
An old New England pasture
Abandoned to peace and time,
And by the magic of beauty
Reclaimed to the sublime.

About it are golden woodlands
Of tulip and hickory;
On the open ridge behind it
You may mount to a glimpse of sea,
The far off, blue, Homeric
Rim of the world's great shield,
A border of boundless glamor
For the soul's familiar field.

In purple and gray-wrought lichen
The boulders lie in the sun;
Along its grassy footpath,
The white-tailed rabbits run.
The crickets work and chirrup
Through the still afternoon;
And the owl calls at twilight
Under the frosty moon.

The odorous wild grape clambers
Over the tumbling wall,
And through the autumnal quiet
The chestnuts open and fall.
Sharing time's freshness and fragrance,
Part of the earth's great soul,
Here man's spirit may ripen
To wisdom serene and whole.

Bliss Carman

The Frost Spirit

He comes, — he comes, — the Frost Spirit comes! You may
    trace his footsteps now
On the naked woods and the blasted fields and the brown
    hill's withered brow.
He has smitten the leaves of the gray old trees where their
    pleasant green came forth,
And the winds, which follow wherever he goes, have shaken
    them down to earth.

He comes, — he comes, — the Frost Spirit comes! from the
    frozen Labrador,
From the icy bridge of the Northern seas, which the white
    bear wanders o'er,
Where the fisherman's sail is stiff with ice and the luckless
    forms below
In the sunless cold of the lingering night into marble statues
    grow!

He comes, — he comes, — the Frost Spirit comes! on the rush-
    ing Northern blast,
And the dark Norwegian pines have bowed as his fearful
    breath went past.
With an unscorched wing he has hurried on, where the fires of
    Hecla glow
On the darkly beautiful sky above and the ancient ice below.

He comes, — he comes, — the Frost Spirit comes! and the
    quiet lake shall feel
The torpid touch of his glazing breath, and ring to the
    skater's heel;
And the streams which danced on the broken rocks, or sang
    to the leaning grass,
Shall bow again to their winter chain, and in mournful silence
    pass.

He comes, — he comes, — the Frost Spirit comes! Let us meet
    him as we may,
And turn with the light of the parlor-fire his evil power
    away;
And gather closer the circle round, when that firelight dances
    high,
And laugh at the shriek of the baffled Fiend as his sounding
    wing goes by!

John Greenleaf Whittier

Photo opposite
FIRST FROST
Ed Cooper

Frost at Midnight

Therefore all seasons shall be sweet to thee,
Whether the summer clothe the general earth
With greenness, or the redbreast sit and sing
Betwixt the tufts of snow on the bare branch
Of mossy apple-tree, while the nigh thatch
Smokes in the sun-thaw; whether the eave-drops fall
Heard only in the trances of the blast,
Or if the secret ministry of frost
Shall hang them up in silent icicles,
Quietly shining to the quiet Moon.

Samuel Taylor Coleridge

Prayer for a Night of Snow

Now in the bleak and frozen night, O Lord,
Loosen the white flakes with a gentle hand,
Sharpen the dark winds lesser than a sword
As they step swiftly down the quiet land.
For I have furry brothers in the fields,
Rabbit and squirrel, chipmunk and the mouse;
Beneath this quarreling sky, the snow it yields,
Give them safe shelter in the forests' house.
Let them find food where snow falls not too deep
Over a thicket of berry, a patch of fern;
Cloak them with comfort and a stretch of sleep.
At daybreak, when the slow horizons burn,
Let all my furry brothers of the night
Stare out, triumphant, on your world of white.

Daniel Whitehead Hicky

Thanksgiving Day

The year decays, November's blast
   Through leafless boughs pipes shrill and drear;
With warmer love the home clasps fast
   The hands, the hearts, the friends most dear.
On many seas men sail the fleet
   Of hopes as fruitless as the foam;
They roam the world with restless feet,
   But find no sweeter spot than home.

Today with quickened hearts they hear
   Old times, old voices chime and call;
The dreams of many a vanished year
   Sit by them at this festival.
Though hearts that warmed them once are cold,
   Though heads are hoar with winter frost
That once were bright with tangled gold —
   Thanks for the blessings kept or lost.

Thanks for the strong, free wind of life,
   However it change or veer;
For the love of mother and sister and wife;
   Clear stars that to haven steer;
For the quenchless lamps of changeless love
   That burn in the night of the dead;
For the life that is, for the hope above,
   Let "thanks" be by all hearts said.

Author Unknown

Give Me a Thankful Heart

God of the winds, the snows, the rains,
   The tides that fall and rise;
The Painter of the vales and plains;
   Lamplighter of the skies;
Thou who has made the land and sea
   And holds them each apart;
Would You but grant me this one plea —
   Give me a thankful heart.

Giver of calm in time of strife,
   Giver of balm in pain;
Thou who alone can give of life
   And take it back again;
Thou who gave of a love that wooed
   And drew this soul apart,
That I might show my gratitude —
   Give me a thankful heart.

God of the atom and its power,
   Wise Keeper of the time;
Guider of men when dark the hour,
   Giver of peace sublime;
Giver of faith that sees the way
   Though heaven and earth depart;
Thou who has given all, I pray —
   Give me a thankful heart.

Donald LaVerne Walker

It's Our
40th Birthday!
IDEALS 1944-1984

We invite you to share with us the wonder of the nativity and the colorful traditions of the holiday season in our next issue, Christmas Ideals.

Marvel at classic paintings by the old masters depicting the beauty and mystery of the birth of Christ.

Reflect on the true meaning of Christmas with writers Charles Dickens, Pearl Buck, and Henry van Dyke.

Delight in Dylan Thomas's nostalgic recollection of "A Child's Christmas in Wales."

Create a gingerbread house to enhance your holiday decor with recipes and house plans provided by us.

All of this (and much more) accompanied by spectacular color photography and original artwork!

Give someone you love an early Christmas gift. Share an Ideals gift subscription with a friend or member of your family, beginning with our Christmas issue.

ACKNOWLEDGMENTS

AUTUMNAL from INTAGLIO by Howard A. Dettmers. THANKSGIVING from LIVING THE YEARS by Edgar A. Guest. Reprinted with permission. PRAYER FOR A NIGHT OF SNOW by Daniel Whitehead Hicky, copyright © 1951 by The New York Times Company. Reprinted by permission. FOR SMALL BLESSINGS from NOT BY BREAD ALONE by Jessie Wilmore Murton, copyright 1969 by Review and Herald Publishing Association. Reprinted with permission. IT'S THANKSGIVING TIME from GRANDFATHER'S FARM by Jessie Wilmore Murton, copyright 1960 by Pacific Press Publishing Association. Reprinted with permission. INDIAN SUMMER from PEN PORTRAITS, copyright 1958 by Maude Woods Plessinger. AN AUTUMNAL TONIC from MORNING, copyright 1907 by James Whitcomb Riley, published by the Bobbs-Merrill Company. The poetry of Margaret Elizabeth Sangster from her books, EASTER BELLS, LITTLE KNIGHTS AND LADIES, and ON THE ROAD HOME, all copyrighted by Harper & Brothers. THANKSGIVING IN BOSTON HARBOR by Hezekiah Butterworth, THE FIRST THANKSGIVING DAY by Alice Williams Brotherton, THANKSGIVING PHILOSOPHY by Charlotte W. Thurston, GIVING THANKS, and THANKSGIVING DAY from OUR AMERICAN HOLIDAYS, THANKSGIVING, edited by Robert Haven Schauffler. THANKSGIVING TIME from HAPPY HOLIDAYS, Volume II, copyright © 1974 by Stella Craft Tremble. GIVE ME A THANKFUL HEART from POEMS WITH A PURPOSE by Donald LaVerne Walker. Our sincere thanks to the following authors whose addresses we were unable to locate: Louise Darcy for THANKSGIVING AT THE FARM and Gloria Ingram Roberts for THANKSGIVING from her book IN WHITE STARLIGHT.